the heart of scripture

GOD WITH US

Les Bridgeman

BIBLEBRIDGE

BibleBridge: Bible Study Lessons
bible-bridge.com

The Heart of Scripture: God with Us
ISBN 978-1543229943

Cover design by Sam Pitts

"And surely I am with you always,

to the very end of the age."

Matthew 28:20

Contents

1.

God with Us in Genesis

Many people who begin reading the Bible never finish. I guess that's understandable since it's a big, ancient book—about one thousand pages long, and two to three thousand years old. Nowadays, not many people read old and thick books.

Reading the entire Bible may intimidate us but understanding it shouldn't. Key themes recur throughout the sacred text and they are not difficult to grasp.

The following pages present the simple theme of God with us as the heart of Scripture. By heart, I mean the core idea that gives energy and life to the rest of the Bible. This reflection and the next three highlight this concept beginning in Genesis and ending in Revelation. The final reflection describes how the reality of God with us should make a difference in our lives.

Adam and Eve

You probably know what it sounds like when a family member walks in the house. You've heard it many times. In Genesis 3, Adam and Eve hear the sound of the LORD God walking in the garden. How often did God walk in that flourishing field? We don't know, but it was enough for them to be familiar with the sound of divine footsteps.

Why was God near Adam and Eve? The answer is not given in Genesis, but it's obvious that the Creator wanted to be close to the humans he created. He didn't form them only to observe them from a distance. His plan was to be involved in their lives. Why? Was God needy and looking for companionship? No, God is love, so God wanted to spend time with Adam and Eve because he loved them, not out of a need in his heart. He wanted them to have the deepest and most fulfilling lives. And he knew in order for them to have that, they needed to be near him.

Enoch and Noah

Although the first humans rebelled against their Creator, and were banished from the garden, God's desire to be with people remained the same. A few chapters later, we see Enoch and then, Noah walking with God (Genesis 5:24; 6:9). There he is again, hanging out with humans. And Enoch and Noah were not merely in God's vicinity; they were living with him in agreement and intimacy—walking with God.

Can you remember a time when you walked with someone and shared intimate things together? Imagine strolling beside God. God did not leave humanity after we turned away from him. As Paul says to the people of Athens who worshiped idols, "he is not far from any one of us" (Acts 17:27).

Abraham, Isaac, and Jacob

God's presence in Genesis continues with Israel's patriarchs, Abraham, Isaac, and Jacob, who lived about four thousand years ago.

- In Genesis 21, Abimelek told Abraham, *"God is with you* in everything you do" (v. 22).[1]
- When Isaac was in Beersheba, the LORD appeared to him and said, "I am the God of your father Abraham. Do not be afraid, for *I am with you*" (26:24).
- In Genesis 28, Jacob had a dream of a staircase reaching to heaven. While angels were ascending and descending the staircase, the LORD stood above it and declared, *"I am with you* and will watch over you wherever you go" (v. 15).

Joseph

Finally, near the end of the Bible's opening book we meet Jacob's son, Joseph. Genesis 39 makes a special point of emphasizing God's presence with Joseph:

- *"The LORD was with Joseph* so that he prospered" (v. 2),
- "But while Joseph was there in the prison, *the LORD was with him*" (v. 21), and

---

[1] Although the story in Genesis 18 is mysterious, it appears that God visited Abraham and Sarah in the form of a human and even ate the meal they prepared. See bible-bridge.com/the-identity-of-the-three-visitors-in-genesis-18.

- *"The LORD was with Joseph* and gave him success in whatever he did" (v. 23).

God's presence gave Joseph success and favor, but it did not keep him from hardship. Joseph was falsely accused and sentenced to prison for about a decade. And during that time God was with him.

Picture a guy in despair for years in an old dungeon. It's dark, lonely, and there's little hope of escaping. Now add God to the scene. God was with Joseph in his misery.

Soon after Joseph was freed, he became one of the rulers of Egypt. And he provided for his family who sought refuge from a famine in Canaan. Before Joseph's father died, he spoke to Joseph and said, "I am about to die, but *God will be with you* and take you back to the land of your fathers" (Genesis 48:21). The *you* in that verse is plural. Jacob (also called Israel) was saying that God would be with all of his descendants and they would return to Canaan.

Conclusion

The God of Genesis wanted to be near the first humans. Even after they rejected him, God still wanted to be with people. The first book of the Bible reveals a God who visited Adam and Eve. And that same God was with Enoch, Noah, Abraham, Isaac, Jacob, and Joseph, in both their good and bad times. Finally, it closes with the promise that God would be with an entire nation—the people of Israel.

2.

God with Us in Israel's History

Have you ever done something you were afraid to do because someone said, "Don't worry, I'll be with you"? Maybe you didn't want to ride a roller coaster, but then a friend said, "I'll go with you" and you found yourself slowly ascending and quickly descending on the track.

I recently went to a zip line course with my family. I didn't want to go, but when my daughters and cousins put on their gear, how could I not join in? And after my youngest daughter readily propelled herself onto the line, how could I remain standing at the base?

We are frequently encouraged to do difficult things because others are with us.

Exodus

In our first reflection, we focused on the references to God accompanying his people in the book of Genesis. About four centuries later, God called Moses to lead Israel out of slavery. But Moses objected, "Who am I, that I should go to Pharaoh and bring the Israelites out of Egypt?"

God replied, "*I will be with you*" (Exodus 3:11–12). There's that theme again: God with his people.

God's words to Moses sound like a parent reassuring a fearful child. Moses would not have to confront Pharaoh alone. The Creator of heaven and earth—the one who was with Adam, Eve, Abraham, and Joseph—promised to be with Moses.

And during his forty years leading Israel, Moses learned the value of God's presence. In Exodus 33, God said, "*My Presence will go with you*, and I will give you rest." And Moses responded,

> If your Presence does not go with us, do not send us up from here. How will anyone know that you are pleased with me and with your people unless *you go with us*? What else will distinguish me and your people from all the other people on the face of the earth? (vv. 14–16).

Moses is saying, "If you don't join us on this journey, we don't want to go." He was convinced that God's presence was the defining feature of the people of Israel.

We can apply this idea to our lives with a simple question: What makes us different? Ultimately, it's not our education or nationality or bank account. The difference-maker is God. God is with us.

Joshua

The sixth book of the Bible opens with Joshua replacing Moses as the new leader of Israel. The LORD promised Joshua, "*As I was with Moses, so I will be with you*; I will never leave you nor forsake you." The LORD continued,

> Be strong and courageous. Do not be terrified; do not be discouraged, for *the LORD your God will be with you wherever you go* (Joshua 1:5–9).

God's presence didn't depart from Israel when Moses died. Instead the same presence that was with Moses remained with Joshua. "*As I was with Moses, so I will be with you.*" God's presence with his people doesn't disappear or even diminish with the passing of time.

While the phrase "I will never leave you nor forsake you" was first spoken to Joshua, it applies to all of God's people. About a thousand years later, the author of Hebrews wrote,

> Keep your lives free from the love of money and be content with what you have, because God has said, "*Never will I leave you; never will I forsake you*" (13:5).

Although God originally spoke those words to Joshua, they apply to the readers of Hebrews a millennium after Joshua, and they apply to us two millennia after Hebrews was written. No matter what we go through or where we end up, God will *never* leave us. And our contentment rests in God's presence.

Judges

As God encouraged Moses and Joshua with his presence, he also encouraged Gideon. While secretly threshing wheat in a winepress out of fear of the foreign invaders, an angel appeared to Gideon and said, "*The LORD is with you*, mighty warrior."

Gideon replied, "But sir, *if the LORD is with us*, why has all this happened to us?" Gideon was thinking, "If God is with us, why am I hiding from an oppressive regime? Why am I using a winepress for wheat?" Instead of answering his question directly, the LORD commanded Gideon to save Israel from Midian. Gideon objected, "Pardon me, my lord . . . but how can I save Israel? My clan is the weakest in Manasseh, and I am the least in my family."

The LORD responded by overruling Gideon's objection with the same words he spoke to Moses, "*I will be with you*" (Judges 6:11–16).

David

King David also understood the importance of God's presence. In Psalm 23 he wrote,

> Even though I walk through the darkest valley,
>
> I will fear no evil,
>
> for *you are with me*;
>
> your rod and your staff,
>
> they comfort me (v. 4).

What gave David courage to go through the darkest places? Two small words in the original Hebrew text, or four simple words in English: *"You are with me."*

Conclusion

God's union with his people wasn't tied to one specific person or one particular generation. God remained with the people of Israel through the centuries. And when his chosen leaders needed encouragement to accomplish a difficult task, he said *"I will be with you."* And he's still saying the same thing to us.

3.

God with Us in Israel's Prophets

Who has been with you during a difficult time? How did that person make a difference by being with you?

I think of friends and family sitting beside each other in a hospital room, students studying together for a big test, and friends talking at a coffee shop.

About ten years ago I went to the hospital for an operation. After checking in, I changed into the medical gown, and then sat down on a bed. While I was waiting, my boss showed up. I was surprised and encouraged to see him. I had been lonely and apprehensive sitting there by myself.

Maybe someone who made a difference for you wasn't even present physically. Maybe that person lived far away, but they answered your phone calls or responded to your emails, listened, and gave advice.

If we are helped by having a friend with us as we face a hardship, how much more so if God is with us?

Our first reflection focused on God with his people in Genesis. The second reflection highlighted that same theme in Exodus, Joshua, Judges, and the Psalms, and we ended with David's words, "I will fear no evil; for *you are with me.*" This reflection centers on what the Hebrew prophets said about God with us.

Isaiah

About two centuries after David, the LORD spoke to Israel through the prophet Isaiah and said,

> When you pass through the waters,
>
> *I will be with you;*
>
> And when you pass through the rivers,
>
> They will not sweep over you.
>
> When you walk through the fire,
>
> You will not be burned;
>
> The flames will not set you ablaze (43:2).

Imagine yourself alone on the bank of a rushing river, fearful, knowing you must get to the other side. Then you hear God's voice:

> When you pass through the waters,
>
> *I will be with you;*
>
> And when you pass through the rivers,
>
> They will not sweep over you.

11

Now step into the water with courage.

Notice that God's words weren't spoken to just one person; they were spoken to an entire nation. God is with us individually *and* corporately and that means *we* as individuals and as a community can "pass through the waters"—the difficult and trying circumstances of life.

The second part of Isaiah 43:2 is dramatically illustrated in the book of Daniel. When the three Jewish exiles in Babylon, Shadrach, Meshach, and Abednego, were thrown into the blazing furnace, the king looked in and saw a fourth person.

> Look! I see four men walking around in the fire, unbound and unharmed, and the fourth looks like a son of the gods. (Daniel 3:25)

Someone joined the trio while they were in the fire. Who? Who would step into the flames with them? Whether it was an angel or the Son of God, the point is the same: God was with them in the fire.

Jeremiah

Around 600 BC, Israel was on the brink of being conquered by the Babylonians when God called a young man named Jeremiah to be his appointed spokesperson or prophet. Jeremiah chapter 1 says,

> The word of the LORD came to me, saying,

"Before I formed you in the womb I knew you, before you were born I set you apart; I appointed you as a prophet to the nations."

"Alas, Sovereign LORD," I said, "I do not know how to speak; I am too young."

But the LORD said to me, "Do not say, 'I am too young.' You must go to everyone I send you to and say whatever I command you. Do not be afraid of them, for *I am with you* and will rescue you,' declares the LORD" (vv. 4–8).

Does that sound familiar? Moses, Gideon, and Jeremiah objected to God's plan for their lives. But each time God responded by promising to be with them. And like he was with Joseph, God was with Jeremiah even when he was in the pit. After being imprisoned, Jeremiah was thrown into an empty cistern where he sank in the mud. But God sent a man to rescue him (chs. 37–39).

Ezekiel

During Jeremiah's time period, Ezekiel lived as one of the exiles in Babylon when God called him to be a prophet. In chapter 10, Ezekiel sees a vision of God's glory departing from the temple in Israel.

So far, in our overview, this is the first example of God leaving his people, or more precisely God's glory departing from the temple. God's departure was devastating because it left Israel defenseless. Why did God leave? Because of his people's rebellion.

But in chapter 43, Ezekiel sees another vision—God returning to the temple and filling it with his glory. God left in judgment, but he returned in mercy. His departure was temporary; his presence is permanent.

Haggai

In 515 BC, the Persian King Cyrus released the exiles from Judah and they returned to the land of Israel. Through the prophet Haggai, the LORD encouraged the returnees to rebuild the temple. Then Haggai gave this message of the LORD to the people: "*I am with you* . . . be strong . . . and work. For *I am with you*" (Haggai 1:13; 2:4).

God was still encouraging Abraham's descendants 1500 years after he had called Abraham. They had experienced slavery in Egypt and an incredible exodus. They had wandered in the wilderness, settled in the land of Canaan, lived under good kings and bad kings, and established the temple only to see it destroyed three centuries later. They were defeated and sent into exile, and seventy years later, they returned to the land. And all the while, God was telling them, *"I am with you."*

With all Israel

In our brief tour, we have come to the end of the Old Testament, but I want to make sure we don't overlook an important point. When exploring this topic it's not enough to highlight the direct statements that God was with his people. In the Hebrew Bible, symbols also play an important role in signifying God's presence. And these symbols show that God was with all of Israel, such as

- the **pillar of fire** at night and the **pillar of cloud** during the day that remained with the people of Israel as they wandered in the wilderness (Exodus 13:21–22),
- the **ark of the covenant**—the rectangular golden box where God told Moses, "*I will meet with you*" (Exodus 25:22),
- the **tabernacle** or tent of God that was set up in the middle of Israel's camp, which God filled with his presence (Exodus 40:34–35), and
- the **temple**—the building in Israel's capital city, Jerusalem, patterned after the tabernacle and dedicated to the worship of Israel's God (1 Kings 8).

Both the tabernacle and temple contain imagery that reminds us of the Garden of Eden where God was with Adam and Eve. For example, they both contained imagery of cherubim and trees with fruit. And they both housed the ark of the covenant— the symbol of the divine presence that was familiar in Eden.

Conclusion

From the beginning of the Old Testament to the end, God encouraged his chosen leaders with his presence. And he showed that he was with Israel through natural phenomena, the tabernacle and temple, and the ark of the covenant. If we were living in ancient Israel we would know that God was with us.

Readers of the Old Testament who miss the theme of God with us, miss one of the most amazing and important parts of the story.

4.

God with Us in Christ

Have you ever been unsure of who to sit beside in a cafeteria? Maybe you grabbed your tray of food and started walking toward a table then realized that you didn't know anyone. Or maybe the people you knew didn't have an open seat beside them. We like to eat with people we know—people we want to talk to, people we want to spend time with.

Eating with Sinners

Choosing the right dinner guests was even more important in the ancient world. People in Israel were extremely picky about their dining company. But not Jesus.

The Pharisees, one of the leading religious groups, were upset when they saw Jesus eating with tax collectors and sinners (Mark 2:15–16). Tax collectors were considered to be traitors and thieves. They worked for the Roman occupiers and they often demanded more money than they were required to collect. Sinners were people who broke God's law either intentionally or unintentionally. Eating with tax collectors and sinners was scandalous behavior to the Pharisees—they would never be seen associating with those kinds of people.

The Pharisees were meticulous in their observance of religious rituals. They studied, they fasted, they attended synagogue and visited the temple, they kept the commandments, and they created their own rules to keep them from breaking the commandments. As with most religious people, their goal was to maintain their focus and purity. So they couldn't even entertain the thought of eating with blatant sinners. They were dedicated to staying set apart from evil influences. The name Pharisee probably means "Separated One."

But Jesus was the "Attached One." Instead of being repelled by wicked people, he was attracted to them. He spent so much time with outcasts that he was derided as "a glutton and a drunkard, a friend of tax collectors and sinners" (Luke 7:34). In Luke 19, he took the initiative to visit a tax collector named Zacchaeus, who hinted at the possibility that he had robbed others (v. 8). When Jesus saw him, he said "I must stay at your house today" (v. 5). And Zacchaeus gladly welcomed him.

Jesus' Prescription

What's going on here? Did Jesus not mind evil? The answer is given in his reply to the Pharisees. When the Pharisees asked, "Why does he eat with tax collectors and sinners?" Jesus responded, "It is not the healthy who need a doctor, but the sick" (Mark 2:17). Jesus viewed sinners as people who were ill. And he saw himself as the doctor who could heal them, so he put on his white coat and went to work. He came "to seek and to save the lost" (Luke 19:10).

Eating with Pharisees

Jesus' behavior offended the Pharisees because they couldn't see their own sinful condition. They avoided external evil, but they failed to recognize the internal evil of pride and hypocrisy. They diagnosed spiritual disease in others, but they gave themselves a clean bill of health.

Jesus saw the Pharisees' condition clearly so he was drawn to heal them as well. While his healing method included strong words of rebuke (see Matthew 23), he also ate with Pharisees. In Luke's Gospel, Jesus received two dinner invitations from a Pharisee, and both times he accepted (7:36; 11:37).

Jesus ate with the religious leaders and "sinners." Jesus is God with *us*—us sinners. Whether our sins are apparent to others or covered up by spiritual pursuits, God wants to spend time with us. He wants to spend time with *anyone* who welcomes him. As he says in the last book of the Bible,

> Here I am! I stand at the door and knock. If anyone hears my voice and opens the door, *I will come in and eat with that person, and they with me* (Revelation 3:20).

Notice the word *anyone*. Jesus will eat with anyone who wants to eat with him. He doesn't discriminate. And notice that he doesn't force himself on us. He takes the initiative by knocking, but he waits for us to open the door.

Jesus' Divine Nature

Jesus' unconventional behavior was a big deal because of who he was. After narrating the angel's message to Joseph about Jesus' birth, Matthew quotes Isaiah's statement, "They will call him Immanuel (which means, God with us)" (Matthew 1:23). The baby who became the young boy, who became the teen-ager, who became the adult, was God with us.

The opening chapter of John makes the same point by asserting that "the Word was with God and the Word was God" (v. 1). "The Word was God." But what else do we know about the Word? Thirteen verses later John states, "The Word became flesh and made his dwelling among us" (v. 14). The Word, who is God, became human and lived with us. And that Word is Christ. As Paul says, "For in Christ the whole fullness of the De-ity lives in bodily form" (Colossians 2:9). God came to be with us in the person of Jesus of Nazareth.

So the big deal with Jesus' behavior is that it's God's behavior. God wants to eat with us. God accepts our dinner invitations. God doesn't discriminate.

Jesus' Suffering

But Jesus didn't come to earth just to have a quick bite with us and then leave. He came to live with us and to experience all of the things we face in a mortal body.

- He grew tired and thirsty from traveling on foot (John 4:6–7).
- He wept at his friend Lazarus's tomb (John 11:35).
- He was tempted like we are (Hebrews 4:15).
- He cried out to be delivered from suffering before his execution (Mark 14:35–36).
- While on the cross, he felt abandoned by God (Mark 15:34).
- And then he died (Mark 15:37).

He fully shared in our humanity (Hebrews 2:14). Jesus is God *with* us—us mortal, suffering humans.

Jesus' Promise

When the time came for Jesus to ascend to his Father he commanded his followers to "go and make disciples of all nations." And just like he assured the patriarchs and Moses and Joshua and Gideon, he assured his disciples, *"I am with you always*, to the very end of the age" (Matthew 28:20). So for the rest of their lives the disciples were confident that Jesus was with them even though they could no longer see him.

About two decades after Jesus ascended to heaven, Paul went to the city of Corinth to share the gospel. But his audience opposed him and even became abusive. The story continues,

> One night the Lord spoke to Paul in a vision: "Do not be afraid; keep on speaking, do not be silent. For *I am with you*, and no one is going to attack

and harm you, because I have many people in this city" (Acts 18:9–10).

Jesus had departed years earlier, but he was still encouraging Paul with the same words he spoke before his ascension.

In addition, notice that Jesus' promise at the end of Matthew says, "to the very end of the age" and not just, "for the rest of your lives." The promise of his presence goes far beyond the life span of the first disciples and Paul. The same Christ that was with them, continues with us today. And he will linger "to the very end of the age."

Jesus' Spirit

But if Jesus departed, how can he be with us? He is with us by his Spirit whom he sent to take his place. He told his followers, "I will ask the Father, and he will give you another advocate to help you and *be with you forever*—the Spirit of truth (John 14:16–17). In Acts 2, the Spirit arrived in dramatic fashion. And now the Spirit is not merely *with* us; the Spirit is *in* us (Romans 8:9–11).

Jesus' Return

While Jesus is with us now by his Spirit, he promised his followers, "I will come back and *take you to be with me* that you also may be where I am" (John 14:3). Thirty years wasn't enough; he wanted to be with his followers forever. And just think of who these followers were.

- They were doubtful—Jesus rebuked them for their lack of faith (Mark 4:40).
- They were proud—arguing about who was the greatest (Mark 9:34).
- They were undisciplined—sleeping when they should have been praying (Mark 14:37).
- They were fearful—running away when Jesus was arrested (Mark 14:50).
- They were disloyal—Peter denied that he knew Jesus (Mark 14:71).

And these are the people that Jesus is going to prepare a place for and the people he wants to be with forever. Jesus wants to be with sinners who welcome him into their lives. And he wants to stay with them, forever.

Jesus' prayer in John 17 gives us a glimpse into his heart. He prayed, "Father, I want those you have given me *to be with me* where I am, and to see my glory" (v. 24). Can you feel his intense desire to be with his people in that statement? "Father, *I want them to be with me.*"

The Book of Revelation

Finally, the Bible ends on a grand crescendo of this theme. After John saw the new heavens, the new earth, and the new Jerusalem coming down from heaven, he heard something.

> And I heard a loud voice from the throne saying, "Look! God's dwelling place is now *among the people*, and *he will dwell with them*. They will be his

people, and *God himself will be with them* and be
their God" (Revelation 21:3).

Three times in that one verse the voice announced that God will make his home with people. There it is—a reason for all of human history, a reason for creation, a reason for suffering, a reason for the cross and resurrection of Christ. So God could be with us.

Conclusion

God with us means God eating and living with sinners like us. It means God with us in our suffering. It means God making his home with us forever. That is the goal of human history. Why? Because God wants to be with us. From Genesis to Revelation, from the Garden of Eden to the eternal city of God, the entire Bible expresses this divine desire.

5.

God with Us: The Difference Maker

In the previous reflections we traced the theme of God with us from the first book of the Bible to the last, from God walking in the Garden of Eden to God making his home with us on earth.

Now let's briefly explore how this theme should make a difference in our lives, beginning with how it should not impact us.

- **It should not make us proud of ourselves.** Perhaps some might think, "If God wants to be with us, we must be something special." But the Adam-and-Eve story shows that we walked away from God. Yet he continued to pursue us. God did not give up on the human race. And the good news of Christ is that "While we were still sinners, Christ died for us" (Romans 5:8). Despite all of our faults, God loves us. And despite the fact that everyone has turned away from God, "he is not far from any one of us" (Acts 17:27). God is with us, not because *we* are great. God is with us because God is love.

- **It should not lead us to think that we will only have success.** God was with Joseph, Moses, David, Jeremiah, and Paul, and every one of them suffered intensely. Joseph was sold as a slave and ended up in prison, Moses wandered in the wilderness for forty years with thousands of complaining people, David had to run for his life from King Saul and his own son, Jeremiah was thrown into a muddy cistern, and Paul was whipped, stoned, and beaten. God with us does not guarantee a pain-free life.

  Don't allow the presence of trouble to cause you to doubt the presence of God. We have the promise of God's presence, but we also have the promise of trouble. Jesus said, "In this world you will have trouble" (John 16:33). Trouble is coming, but God will be with us. When King Nebuchadnezzar saw Shadrach, Meshach, and Abednego in the blazing furnace, he saw someone else with them. As God promised in Psalm 91, "*I will be with him in trouble*" (v. 15). God is with us, and if something bad happens to us, God is *still* with us.

- **It should not lead us to think that how we live doesn't matter.** Some may think, "God is with us no matter what, so what we do doesn't matter." But the New Testament contains many warnings about how we should live. For example, after listing the acts of the flesh, Paul wrote, "I warn you, as I did before, that those who live like this will not inherit the kingdom of God" (Galatians 5:21).

The theme of God with us should impact us in the following ways.

- **It should make us want to be with God.** When we realize how much God wants to be with us, it should make us want to reciprocate that desire. Paul said, "I desire to depart and *be with Christ*, which is better by far" (Philippians 1:23).

- **It should give us courage to do hard things and to endure hardship.** David wrote, "Even though I walk through the darkest valley, I will fear no evil, for *you are with me*" (Psalm 23:4). God's presence should give us confidence to face difficult circumstances. "When you pass through the waters, *I will be with you*" (Isaiah 43:2).

- **It should give us contentment with what we have.** "Keep your lives free from the love of money and be content with what you have, because God has said, '*Never will I leave you; never will I forsake you*'" (Hebrews 13:5). We have God's presence, what are we running after?

- **It should cause us to rejoice.** God wants to be with us. God enjoys our company. Isn't that an incredible thought? God is not against us; "God is for us" (Romans 8:31). I can't think of a more fitting conclusion to these reflections than the words of John Wesley. On his deathbed, with the little strength he had left, Wesley fervently spoke his final words, repeating the same thing twice.

"The best of all is, God is with us.

The best of all is, God is with us."

Other Books by Les Bridgeman

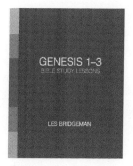

The first three chapters of Genesis set the stage for the entire Bible. In these opening pages we meet God, Adam, Eve, the animals, and all of the elements that compose our world. We also see a picture of every human—how we are tempted and how we succumb to temptation. In addition, Genesis 1–3 have been at the center of much scientific controversy. What are the different views and various interpretations? *Genesis 1–3: Bible Study Lessons* guides readers through these fascinating and challenging chapters. Written for ages 14 and up, this study contains 23 lessons, 3 quizzes, 1 test, and an answer key.

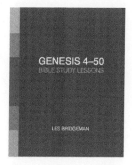

In this companion volume to *Genesis 1–3: Bible Study Lessons*, we meet the patriarchs and matriarchs of Israel's faith. Their stories are filled with intense human drama: sibling rivalries, murder, abduction, romance, passionate prayer, fierce wrestling, meaningful dreams, betrayal, and false accusation. But through their lives we see God's faithfulness from one generation to the next even during a great flood and severe famine. Written for ages 14 and up, *Genesis 4–50: Bible Study Lessons* contains 34 lessons, 3 quizzes, 3 tests, and an answer key.

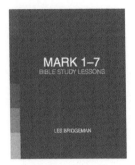

In Mark 1–7, Jesus emerges as a powerful healer, deliverer, and teacher. He speaks with authority as he drives out evil spirits, calms storms, and heals the sick. But he's more than just a miracle worker. He's a rule breaker. He touches a leper, eats with the wrong crowd, and rebukes the rule enforcers for their hypocrisy. He prefers to show compassion and stand for truth than to follow human traditions. Written for ages 14 and up, *Mark 1–7: Bible Study Lessons* contains 33 lessons, 4 quizzes, 2 tests, and an answer key.

Seeing the Invisible God: 52 Biblical Reflections on Divine Anatomy provides a unique and insightful journey through the Bible and Christian theology. By focusing on the biblical references to divine anatomy (e.g., God's face, eyes, ears, hand, etc.), the 52 reflections offer solid biblical content, a deep devotional emphasis, and engagement with key translation and theological challenges.

For new releases visit bible-bridge.com.

Made in the USA
Coppell, TX
30 June 2021

58364071R00023